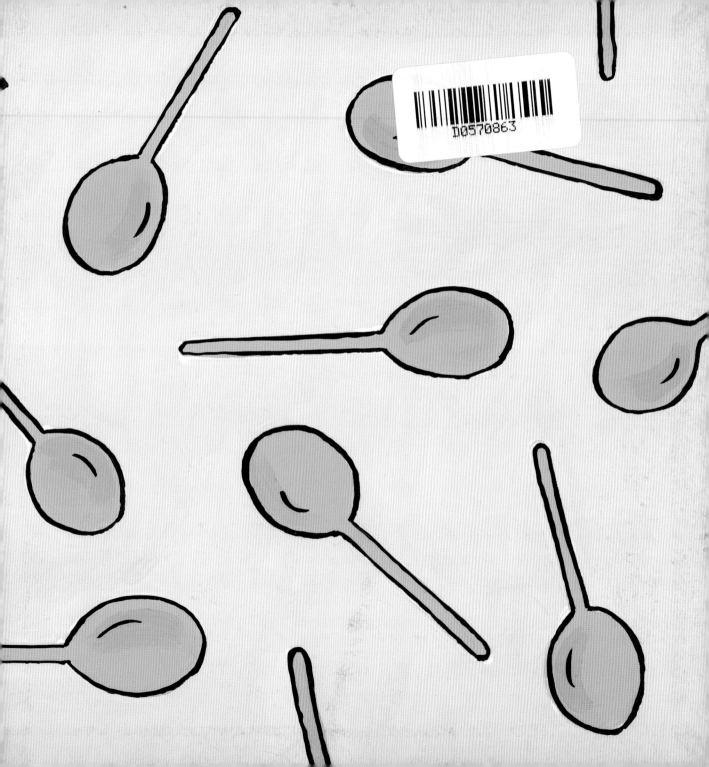

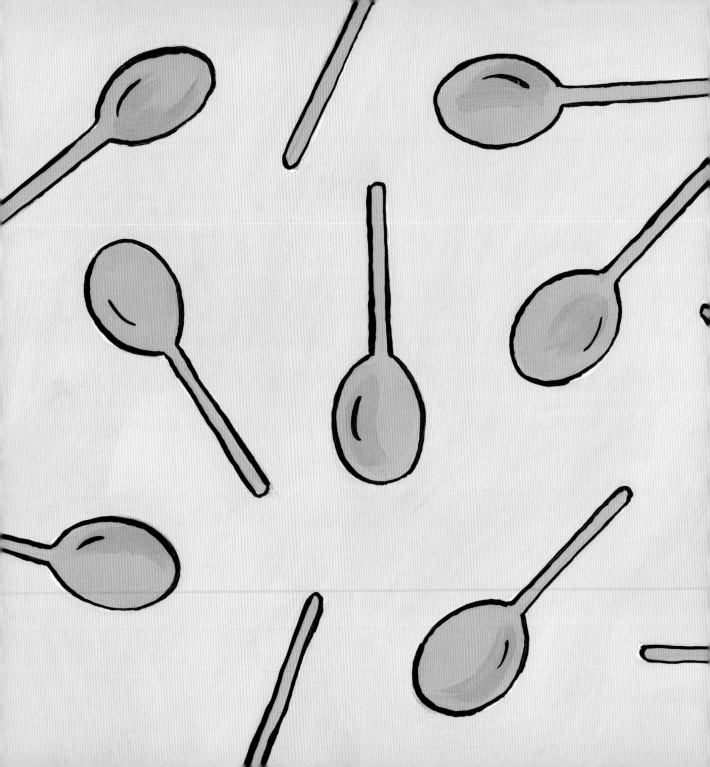

Dear Parents,

Children's earliest experiences with stories and books usually involve grown-ups reading to them. However, reading should be active, and as adults, we can help young readers make meaning of the text by prompting them to relate the book to what they already know and to their personal experiences. Our questions will lead them to move beyond the simple story and pictures and encourage them to think beneath the surface. For example, after reading a story about the sleep habits of animals, you might ask, "Do you remember when you moved into a big bed? Could you see the moon out of your window?"

Illustrations in these books are wonderful and can be used in a variety of ways. Your questions about them can direct the child to details and encourage him or her to think about what those details tell us about the story. You might ask the child to find three different "beds" used by animals and insects in the book. Illustrations can even be used to inspire readers to draw their own pictures related to the text.

At the end of each book, there are some suggested questions and activities related to the story. These questions range in difficulty and will help you move young readers from the text itself to thinking skills such as comparing and contrasting, predicting, applying what they learned to new situations and identifying things they want to find out more about. This conversation about their reading may even result in the children becoming the storytellers, rather than simply the listeners!

Harriet Ziefert, M.A.
Language Arts/Reading Specialist

More to **Think** About

Does a Woodpecker Use a Hammer?

Does a Bear Wear Boots?

Does a Beaver Sleep in a Bed?

Does a Panda Go to School?

Does an Owl Wear Eyeglasses?

Does a Tiger Go to the Dentist?

Doe a Hippo Go to the Doctor?

Does a Seal Smile?

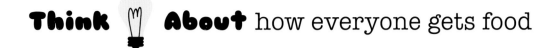
Does a **Camel** **Cook** Spaghetti?

Harriet Ziefert • illustrations by **Emily Bolam**

BLUE APPLE

Text copyright © 2007, 2014 by Harriet Ziefert
Illustrations copyright © 2007 by Emily Bolam
All rights reserved
CIP data is available.
Published in the United States 2014 by
🍎 Blue Apple Books
515 Valley Street, Maplewood, NJ 07040
www.blueapplebooks.com
Printed in China
ISBN: 978-1-60905-422-9
1 3 5 7 9 10 8 6 4 2
02/14

Does a camel cook?

No. A camel doesn't cook!

Camels eat grass and leaves.
They can go for a month without food.

Does a squirrel cook?

Of course not. A squirrel doesn't cook.

Squirrels gather nuts and seeds.
They eat some and store the rest for the winter.

Does a bear cook?

Don't be silly.
Bears eat fish, nuts, berries, and honey.
If they eat meat, they don't cook it.

Does a raccoon cook?

No way!
Raccoons eat just about
everything—fish, fruit, nuts,
and even garbage.

Raccoons wash their
food with water
before they eat it.
If they can't find
water, they "wash"
their food without it.

Does a chimp cook?

No, chimps don't cook.

Unlike other animals, chimps can use tools to find food.
A chimp can use a piece of grass to fish termites
out of a hole in the ground.
But a chimp can't cook those termites!

All animals eat, but only humans cook their food.

Humans grow fruits and vegetables
on farms or in gardens.

They raise animals for meat and milk.

Humans use many different tools
to help them prepare their food—knives, forks,
spoons, pots, pans, stoves, and ovens.

People in different countries prepare different kinds of foods.

In Italy, they prepare a lot of pasta, such as spaghetti or ravioli.

In Japan, they make sushi, which is raw fish and rice wrapped in seaweed.

In India, they cook curry using vegetables and spices.

In America, many people like to eat
hot dogs and hamburgers and french fries.

Animals have to eat what they
can find in their territory.

Giraffes and elephants eat
leaves and twigs from
the tops of trees.

But you won't find them eating watermelon,
because it doesn't grow where they live.

Many people in the world eat the food they
grow, or hunt, or find themselves.

But people in some countries can shop
at grocery stores to find food from all over the world.

Your dinner could come from a farm next door
or from a place far across the world.

People can even order special foods online
when they can't find them in a store.

What do you like to eat?
Where does it come from?

Think 💡 About how everyone gets food

This book compares the eating behaviors of squirrels, bears, raccoons, and chimps to the ways that people grow and prepare the food they eat.

Compare and Contrast

- Choose an animal that lives near where you live: a pigeon, a duck, a goose, a worm, an ant. Find out what the animal eats and how it finds food.
- What are some things animals eat that you like to eat?
- What are some things animals eat that you would not want to eat?

Research

Go to a library or online and find out:

- how a mother bird feeds her babies
- how a mother cat feeds her babies
- how a mother whale feeds her babies
- How much does a bird eat? A cow eat? An elephant eat? A snake eat?
- How often do these animals eat? Once a day? Once a week? Three meals a day?

Choose a country you are curious about.

Look in the library to find out, or ask someone who has lived there, what they usually eat for lunch in that country.

Go to the Animals Section of your library.

Pull out some interesting books. Read about how and what different animals eat.

Observe

When you are eating a meal, direct your attention to others eating with you.

- Do people use their knives and forks differently?
- How do they use their napkins?
- How do they chew and swallow?

Do you know any babies?

Watch them eat. How do they get food to their mouth?

What's the difference between how the baby eats and the way a toddler eats?

Watch someone cook.

- What foods were cooked?
- What tools were used to prepare the food?
- Ask the cook where the food came from. From your state? From outside the U.S.?

Write, Tell, or Draw

Imagine the perfect cupcake.
Write a recipe for it and include a picture. Will the cupcake be served at a party? Tell us about that delicious event!

Write a menu for your favorite meal.
Is your favorite breakfast, lunch, or dinner? Add pictures of the food!

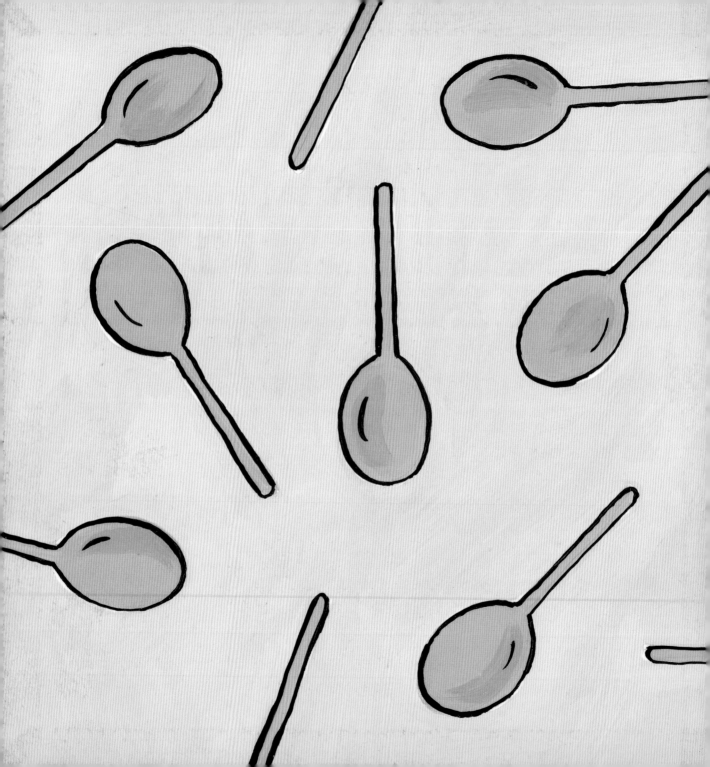